AF545157

The Second Continental Congress

Bonnie Hinman

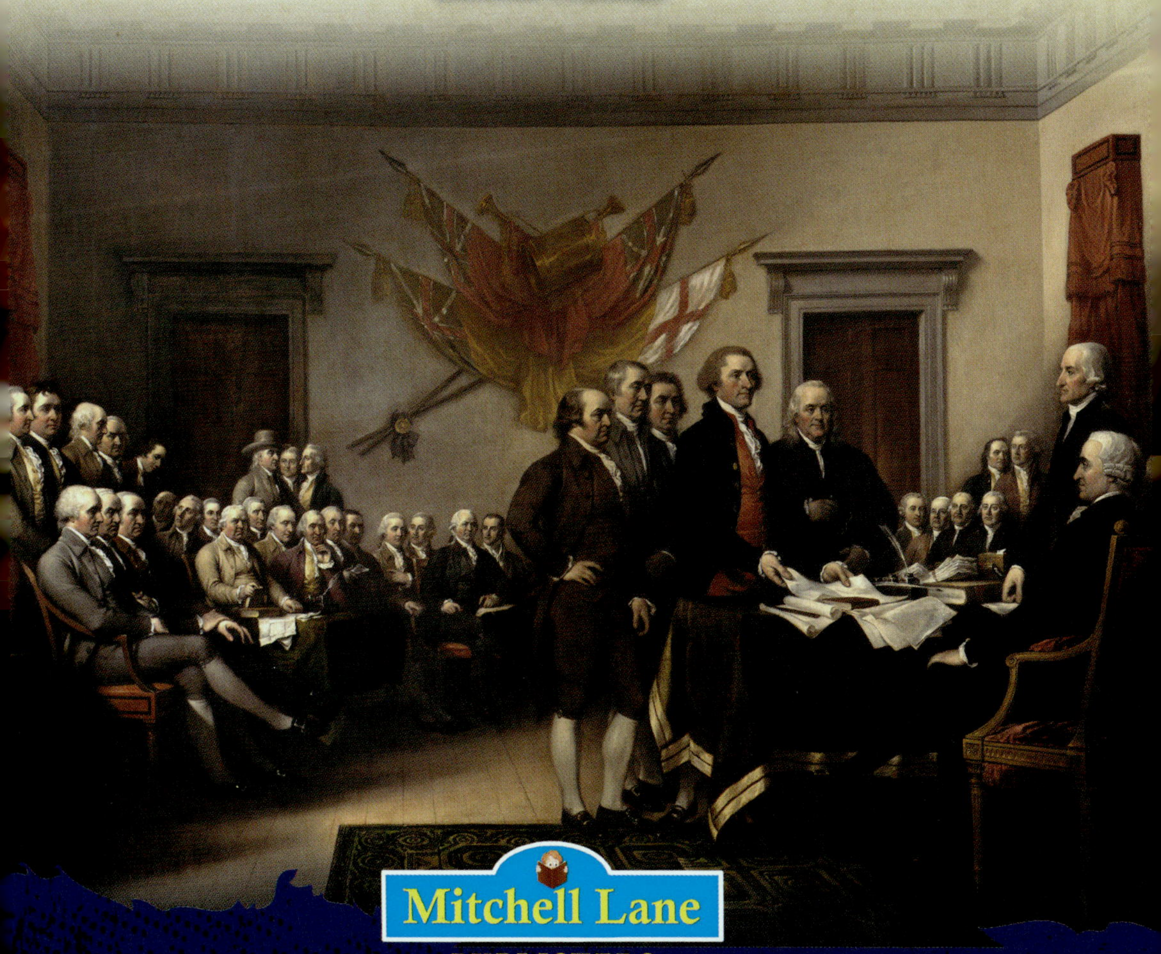

Mitchell Lane
PUBLISHERS
2001 SW 31st Avenue
Hallandale, FL 33009
www.mitchelllane.com

Copyright © 2018 by Mitchell Lane Publishers. All rights reserved. No part of this book may be reproduced without written permission from the publisher. Printed and bound in the United States of America.

Printing 1 2 3 4 5 6 7 8

The First Continental Congress
The French and Indian War
Life in the Original 13 Colonies
The Second Continental Congress
The Signers of the Declaration of Independence
Stamp Act Congress
The Story of the Declaration of Independence
An Overview of the American Revolution

Library of Congress Cataloging-in-Publication Data
Names: Hinman, Bonnie, author.
Title: The second Continental Congress / by Bonnie Hinman.
Description: Hallandale, FL : Mitchell Lane Publishers, [2018] | Series: Young America | Includes bibliographical references and index. | Audience: Ages 9-13. | Audience: Grades 7-8.
Identifiers: LCCN 2017009125 | ISBN 9781612289793 (library bound)
Subjects: LCSH: United States. Continental Congress—History—Juvenile literature. | United States—Politics and government—1775-1783—Juvenile literature. | United States—History—Revolution, 1775-1783—Juvenile literature.
Classification: LCC E303 .H587 2018 | DDC 973.3—dc23
LC record available at https://lccn.loc.gov/2017009125

eBook ISBN: 978-1-61228-980-9

Words in **bold** throughout can be found in the Glossary.

King George III was the King of England before, during, and after the Revolutionary War. After the American colonies were lost, George's popularity fell. In 1788, George suffered through an episode of insanity. He eventually recovered but had recurrences of the illness for the rest of his life. He is often called "Mad King George."

1

Stamp Acts and Tea Parties

Sometimes the **sequel** to a movie or book is not nearly as good as the original. That wasn't the case when the Second Continental Congress met in 1775, less than a year after the First Continental Congress had adjourned. As it turned out, there was even more excitement for the Second Congress and more than enough originality. The sequel to the First Continental Congress gave birth to the United States.

In 1775, the American colonies had existed under British rule for many years. For almost that entire time, the colonies and Great Britain got along just fine. Britain set some restrictions on the colonies and charged certain taxes. However, they hadn't made much of an effort to enforce the restrictions or collect the taxes.

Everything began to change after the French and Indian War ended in 1763. Though Britain won the conflict, it was deeply in debt for the costs of the fighting. King George III and the British Parliament decided that the American colonies should help pay this debt.

Most Americans were loyal to their king and mother country. But when the king and Parliament began to pass new taxes and trade **restrictions**, the colonists grumbled, complained, and protested.

Stamp Act

The best-known of these new taxes was the Stamp Act. Passed by Parliament in March 1765, the Stamp Act required that colonists purchase special stamps for all legal documents and a variety of other printed materials. Specially appointed collectors would sell these stamps.

Historian Edmund Cody Burnett wrote of the Stamp Act, "A big lump of fat had been thrown into the fire, with the result that there was soon much sizzling."[1] Protests broke out in the colonies. In October 1765, representatives of nine colonies met in New York for the Stamp Act Congress. The representatives agreed that Parliament was taxing the colonies without the colonies having any say in the matter.

The Act was supposed to go into effect November 1, 1765, but colonists staged public demonstrations against it. On that day stamp collectors stayed home, and there were barely any stamps for sale.

Meanwhile, Parliament was rethinking its strategy. In January 1766 it **repealed** the Stamp Act. At the same time, it voted to give itself supreme authority over the colonies. Parliament particularly wanted to control trade.[2]

Several years went by as Britain imposed first one restriction then another on the colonies' trade. There were import duties on incoming goods and rules about where American raw materials and products could be exported.

Boston Tea Party

The pot of simmering anger against all of these restrictions eventually boiled over in Boston in December 1773, when the Boston Tea Party took place. According to the

recently passed Tea Act, the East India Company would ship tea directly from India to the colonies to save on shipping costs. On paper it looked like tea would cost less. However, American merchants would pay new taxes on the tea. Parliament also gave the East India Company a **monopoly** on the tea trade in the colonies. They could raise prices any time they desired.[3]

Many colonists were already buying tea **smuggled** in from Holland and paying no taxes at all. Smuggled tea was cheaper. The prospect of higher prices was alarming.

The Sons of Liberty were a secret Boston organization of patriots. Samuel Adams led other members in dressing up as Indians and swarming aboard East India Company ships in Boston Harbor as they waited to be unloaded. The "Indians" dumped the tea overboard.[4]

Parliament fumed over this action and in spring of 1774 passed what the colonies called the **Intolerable** Acts. Many of these Acts carried harsh penalties for Massachusetts. Boston had to repay the East India Company for the tea

The destruction of the tea in Boston Harbor came to be called the Boston Tea Party. The British government was shocked by the actions of the colonists. King George III was determined to punish Boston and the whole colony of Massachusetts for this act.

thrown overboard or the harbor would be closed even to fishing boats. Britain would take over governing Massachusetts, and colonists could be required to keep British soldiers in their homes.[5]

Boston refused to pay for the tea, and the harbor was closed on June 1. With the Stamp Act Congress in mind, colonial leaders decided to meet in Philadelphia. They hoped to find a solution to the problems in Boston. By late August, representatives of every colony except Georgia had made the trek to Philadelphia. They met in Carpenters' Hall on September 5 for the historic First Continental Congress.

First Continental Congress

Independence was not on the minds of the delegates. Many of them even thought that Boston should pay for the tea. But most also thought that the closing of Boston Harbor and the other Intolerable Acts were too harsh. They wanted fair treatment for Boston and the other colonies. They wanted freedom to trade with other countries. Above all they wanted British General Thomas Gage to take his thousands of troops out of Boston.

The delegates believed that a reasonable approach to King George and Parliament would cause the British to repeal the Intolerable Acts. Britain had backed down about the Stamp Act. Maybe they would do the same for these acts.

The First Continental Congress debated how to get Britain to repeal the Intolerable Acts. The delegates didn't agree much of the time. Though they were controlled by Britain, they had different problems and needs. Each one wanted to solve its own problems with Britain first.

By the end of October, the delegates had hammered out some compromises. Congress sent letters to citizens in Britain, Canada, and the colonies. These letters explained

Payton Randolph of Virginia was easily elected chairman, or president, of the First Continental Congress. However, there was much argument and debate over who should be secretary of the Congress. Charles Thomson of Pennsylvania was finally elected to that post.

the **grievances** that the delegates felt they had against Britain. The delegates signed a plan called the Continental Association that called for a boycott against British goods. The delegates labored and argued over a letter to King George. This letter spelled out the problems, and asked for the king's help to resolve the issues.[6]

The First Continental Congress adjourned on October 26, 1774. The delegates agreed that they would meet again on May 10 the following year if Britain hadn't solved the problems. Massachusetts delegate John Adams wrote in his diary on October 28, "It is not very likely that I shall ever see this Part of the World again, but I shall ever retain a most greatfull, pleasing Sense, of the many Civilities I have received, in it."[7]

It turned out that Adams would have every opportunity to receive many more civilities from Philadelphia in the years to come.

In 1774, British General Thomas Gage was appointed military commander and royal governor of the Massachusetts Colony. He sent soldiers to collect gunpowder that was stored at different places around the countryside. He wanted to prevent the colonists from fighting with government officials. Instead, he caused the first shots of the Revolutionary War to be fired. In April 1775, he sent soldiers to capture gunpowder at Concord, Massachusetts. This mission led to the famous Battle of Lexington and Concord.

2

Return to Philadelphia

The world was different when the delegates **convened** again in May 1775 as the Second Continental Congress. If they had been hopeful in October, they were not now.

Their letter to King George did not get a good reception. The letter had wished the king "a long and glorious reign over loyal and happy subjects."[1] The king had already received word that the Massachusetts colony was stirring up trouble. He wasn't in the mood to read a letter from subjects who obviously weren't loyal or happy.

In a letter to one of his government ministers, King George wrote, "The New England governments are in a state of rebellion, blows must decide whether they be subject to this country or independent."[2]

Many colonial leaders still hoped Great Britain might back down. Delegates were getting ready to leave for Philadelphia when the first blow struck. General Gage planned a brief operation to seize some gunpowder stored in Concord, a town near Boston, in the early hours of April 19. He also hoped to arrest troublemakers Samuel Adams and John Hancock as a show of authority.

Gage's operation didn't go as planned. Warned by Paul Revere and other riders, the militia turned out in force. The two sides confronted each other at dawn in the village of Lexington. Each side blamed the other for firing the first shot. What followed was a long day of gunfire. Seventy-three British soldiers died, along with forty-nine colonial militia members. The British soldiers limped back to Boston while Samuel Adams and John Hancock left for Philadelphia.

Paul Revere did not become famous right away for his 1775 ride to Lexington. Fame came after poet Henry Wadsworth Longfellow wrote "Paul Revere's Ride" in 1861. Longfellow used a few facts and much imagination to write the famous poem that begins, "Listen my children, and you shall hear of the midnight ride of Paul Revere."

The Second Continental Congress Meets

Philadelphia residents noisily welcomed the returning delegates, with thousands of people marching to **fifes** and drums and cheering them. News of the Battle of Lexington and Concord had traveled quickly. Colonists wanted action against Britain.

The Second Continental Congress convened on May 10. Routine business came first and then debate began about the April 19 battle. Delegate Richard Henry Lee of Virginia proposed that the colonies raise an army immediately. He wanted a "continental army" rather than individual colonial militias. This idea met strong opposition from some colonial delegations. They thought that raising a continental army would signal to Great Britain that they were ready to go to war.[3]

Richard Henry Lee was one of the founders of the Committees of Correspondence in the American colonies. These committees were set up to allow the colonies to communicate with each other in their opposition to the British.

Pennsylvania delegate John Dickinson led the opposition. He didn't want an army or independence from Britain. Despite the events at Lexington and Concord, he still hoped to avoid war.

Dickinson said that the result of such a war would leave "many valuable lives lost that might be saved & much other Destruction that might perhaps be prevented. . . . We have not yet tasted deeply of that bitter

Cup called the Fortunes of War."[4] Dickinson felt that every possible effort to avoid such a devastating war should be made.

Congress Raises an Army

While many delegates agreed that they wanted to avoid war, they also believed that they had to defend themselves. On June 14, Congress voted to establish the Continental Army. Massachusetts and New York would provide most of the men, and Congress would pay them. Where Congress would get the money to support this army was not clear. The Congress had no power to make the colonies pay the soldiers.

On June 15, Congress appointed George Washington as commanding general of those forces. Washington was one of the few men in America with a reputation as a military leader. He had served during the French and Indian War as the commander of the Virginia militia. Washington left for Boston on June 22 to take command of the existing forces and begin **recruitment** of many more men.

Even as Washington was appointed as commanding general, trouble was brewing in Massachusetts. Patriot spies reported that General Gage planned to occupy a strategic position in the hills around Dorchester, south of Boston. The New England militia responded to this plan with one of their own. They took over the Charlestown peninsula north of Boston. The peninsula was dominated by two hills, Breed's Hill and Bunker Hill.

The Battle of Bunker Hill

What became known as the Battle of Bunker Hill began on June 17. British ships in the harbor rained fire on the militia, which had hastily dug earth **fortifications**. General

Soldiers of the Continental Army wore a great variety of uniforms. When the war began, many experienced soldiers put on the uniforms they had worn in the French and Indian War. Washington preferred a simple hunting shirt and breeches but other leaders wanted a more fashionable look. Commanders preferred troops who looked the same to easily identify them on smoky battlefields. But a clothing shortage throughout the war made it hard for uniforms to be the same. Eventually most uniform coats were blue as seen here. But they could still vary year-by-year and by regiment.

Gage ordered a direct attack on Breed's Hill. The Americans beat back two assaults by the British troops. A third assault near the end of the day found the defenders nearly out of gunpowder. They had to retreat.

British forces took the two hills but both sides paid a high price. The British had 226 soldiers killed, including many officers. The Americans lost 140 men. Most of the

During the Battle of Bunker Hill, the colonists fought from pits they had dug on the top of Breed's Hill. The British used a line infantry type of charge against the Americans. British soldiers advanced up the hill in lines or ranks. The first line would fire at the same time and then drop back to reload. The second line would advance to fire and then drop back. It was a bloody way to fight but most European armies used this method until the mid-1800s.

American casualties happened during the retreat. Washington was angry that the militia had run out of gunpowder. He immediately sent a message to Congress asking them to send **munitions** as soon as possible. This was the first of many requests that Washington made to Congress. A **chronic** shortage of supplies and the money to pay for them became an ongoing source of frustration for him.[5]

Word had previously reached Congress that New Hampshire militia leader Ethan Allen and his forces had captured Fort Ticonderoga in northern New York. This news encouraged Congress even though they hadn't ordered the attack. On June 27, they appointed Philip Schuyler, a New York delegate, as a major general and encouraged him to advance into Canada from Fort Ticonderoga in the first major American military operation. Congress believed that Canada was lightly defended by the British, and were optimistic that the continental troops would be victorious. That would open the door for Canada to become the 14th American colony.

In Philadelphia, John Dickinson pushed forward a motion to send another petition to King George. He still hoped to work out the differences between the colonies and their mother country. The debate was tension-filled. Why send another petition since George had rejected the first one, some delegates wondered.

However, the motion passed, and the petition, written mostly by Dickinson, went on its way to Britain. In it Dickinson described the Americans as "Majesty's faithful Subjects." The petition closed, "Your Majesty, that your royal authority and influence may be graciously interposed to procure us relief."[6] Later this petition would be called the Olive Branch Petition. It was the last plea sent to the king asking for **reconciliation**.

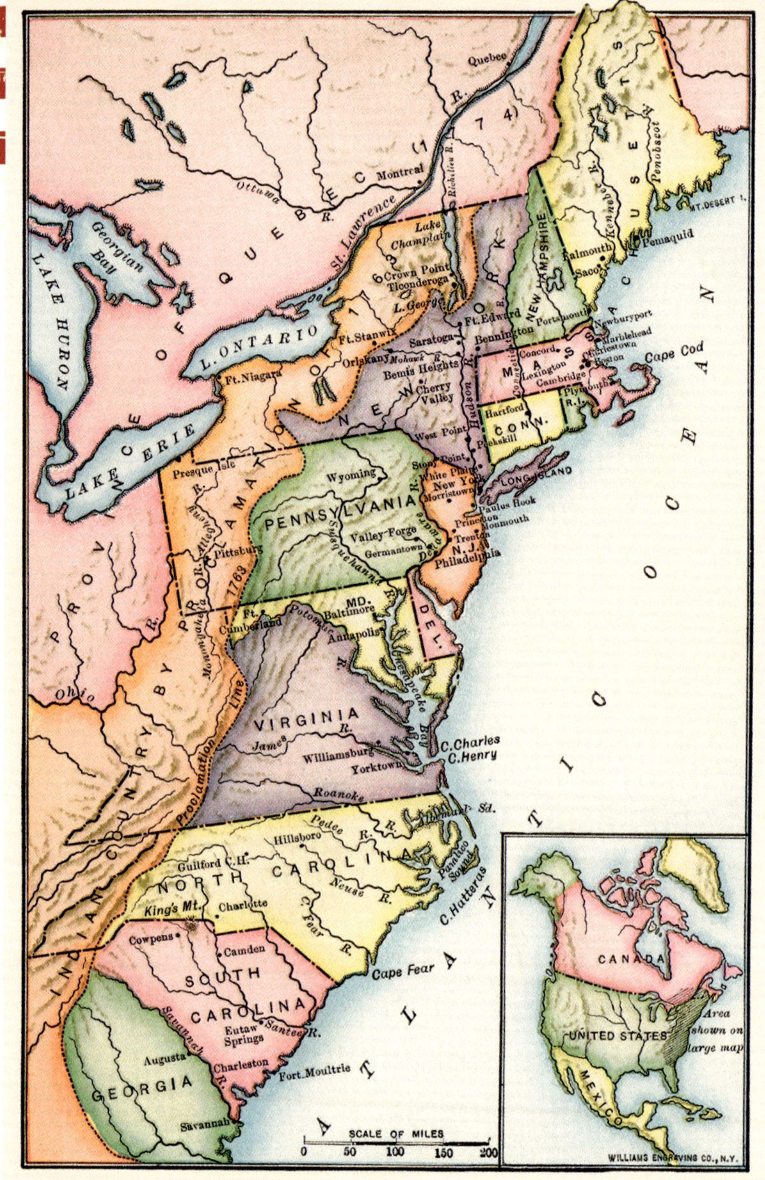

The thirteen colonies at the beginning of the Revolution stretched from New Hampshire in the north to Georgia in the south. Several of the northern colonies bordered Canada, which was British territory. In the south, Georgia bordered Florida, which was Spanish territory. Maine, Florida, and Vermont were eventually added to the new country.

3

Running the War

The delegates were hot and tired by the end of June. Philadelphia was having its usual hot summer, and the men began to think of returning to their homes. However, there was still business.

Congress ordered the printing of paper money to pay for the supplies that General Washington continued to ask for. They lifted some of the **prohibitions** on imports so gunpowder and muskets could be obtained. A continental postal system was established. Congress dispatched messages to the main Indian tribes, assuring them that the colonists had no quarrel with them and asking them not to side with the British. The delegates approved a hospital establishment plan, along with salaries for all needed employees.[1]

Delegates began going home by the end of July. Congress rushed through the last business on the morning of August 2. Connecticut delegate Eliphalet Dyer's letter to a friend probably summed up the feelings of all of the delegates: "We are all exhausted sitting so long in this place and being so long confined together that we feel pretty much as a Number of passengers confined together on board ship for a long Voyage."[2]

Their work was hardly done. They began straggling back to Philadelphia in early September. On September 13, they called the Congress to order.

Since the Continental Congress had no real power other than what the colonies agreed to give it, they ran their business by committee. Every issue or problem required a committee. Sometimes a new committee was formed to give instructions to one already in existence. It was not an efficient way to run a government or war, but without a chief executive it seemed the fairest way to manage business.

During the entire year of 1775, Congress appointed 59 committees. In the first week after reconvening in September alone, more than a dozen committees were established. Among them were committees to study trade, buy uniforms for the army, and pay the bills. There was even a committee to answer General Washington's many letters containing requests and registering complaints about the Continental Army he had taken over.[3]

General Washington's Army

The state of the Continental Army was a problem in the fall of 1775. The army Washington took over in June consisted mostly of Massachusetts militia members. He had found a sad lack of discipline and **resolve** in those troops. They were untrained soldiers with no experience of the discipline required of a regular army. At one point, Washington ordered his soldiers to stop firing their muskets in the air for no reason. He also ordered them not to bathe near a bridge in Cambridge, a town across the Charles River from Boston. Residents complained that the soldiers were running on the bridge naked.[4]

George Washington formally took command of the American army on July 3, 1775, in Cambridge, Massachusetts. Washington drew his sword in front of the assembled troops. This gesture indicated that he was willing to take on the difficult job of leading the army.

Washington complained vigorously about the officers appointed for him. According to his letters, many of his officers were **incompetent**, sometimes cowardly, and often broke the law.

A Congressional committee visited Washington's camp in Cambridge to investigate his complaints. The committee's report strongly urged better pay for the soldiers. They also recommended a tighter military code of behavior to help discipline. These actions helped Washington manage his army, and conditions improved a little by the end of 1775.

More committees looked into creating an American Navy. In October, the Congress approved the purchase of two vessels and the guns to outfit them. By the end of December, Congress had approved the outfitting of 14 additional ships. They also established two battalions of marines to serve on those ships.[5]

King George and the Olive Branch

The delegates believed that King George was considering the Olive Branch Petition sent to him in July. The man dispatched to take the petition to Britain arrived there on August 13, but for unknown reasons the delivery to the king didn't happen until sometime in September. If the petition had ever had a chance to sway King George, it was too late by then. He refused to even look at the document and made no reply.

The Congress didn't know that news of the Battle of Bunker Hill had reached Britain in July. The king was outraged and planned to take new actions against the rebellious colonies. He was convinced that they would eventually bend to Britain's authority.

On August 23, King George issued a Proclamation for Suppressing Rebellion and Sedition. In the King's proclamation, he said the colonies were in a state of "open and **avowed** rebellion."[6]

News of the King's proclamation and rejection of the Olive Branch Petition didn't reach Congress until the second week of November. Discouraging as this news was, some members of Congress still hoped to find a way to avoid war.

Lord Dunmore's Army

In the final weeks of 1775, the war reached Virginia. The royal governor of Virginia, the Earl of Dunmore, had sent

a small force to attack the Virginia militia near Norfolk, Virginia. The Virginians crushed the earl's army in a battle lasting less than 30 minutes.

The earl had recruited some of his soldiers by promising freedom to any slaves or indentured servants who would join him. This invitation disturbed Virginians and other southerners. They needed their slaves and servants to labor on their farms and in their businesses. Hundreds of runaway slaves enlisted in Dunmore's army, but their lack of training made defeat certain for Dunmore's army.[7]

Delegates worked right up until the last day of the year, took December 31 off, and came back to work on January 1. They had no way of knowing that 1776 would be perhaps the most memorable year in American history.

Lord Dunmore continued his fight against the Virginia militia after his defeat at Norfolk. He moved to Gwynn's Island near Norfolk but his troops suffered from smallpox and other diseases. Eventually, he was forced to flee to New York and then back to England where he was a staunch supporter of the fight against the Americans.

Englishman Thomas Paine was most famous for writing the pamphlet *Common Sense*. It is credited with helping convince Americans to rebel against Britain. Paine also wrote another pamphlet called *The American Crisis* after traveling with the American army. It contains the well-known quote, "These are the times that try men's souls."

4

Common Sense Persuades

The dawning of the exciting year of 1776 was anything but exciting for the delegates of the Second Continental Congress. Discouraging news seemed to arrive daily during January. Lord Dunmore launched a naval attack on Norfolk, Virginia. The city burned.

The news from Britain included the speech King George had given to Parliament the previous October. The king strongly rejected all of the colonists' ideas for compromise. Only John Dickinson and a few other delegates could see any hope for avoiding war. The king had offered to forgive any colonists who would turn from their rebellious ways. Dickinson saw a small chance in that offer that the King would be willing to negotiate.[1]

February brought the news that Parliament had passed the Prohibitory Act. Any ships found trading with the colonies would have their cargoes **confiscated**. The Act went into effect on January 1, before the colonies even knew about it. This was the beginning of the war at sea.

Thomas Paine

In the midst of a bad winter, there was one bright spot. Thomas Paine's *Common Sense* pamphlet was published in Philadelphia. This pamphlet had a profound influence on the colonists, by helping to convince them that independence was the only answer. It probably swayed the colonists more than any fancy speeches or debates in the Continental Congress.

Thomas Paine had moved from London to Philadelphia in 1774. He wanted a fresh start. His career as an exciseman or tax collector had not ended well after he tried to help his fellow excisemen get a pay raise. His first wife and child had died and his second wife deserted him. But he had met Benjamin Franklin, who provided Paine with a letter of introduction. This letter plus a settlement paid him by his second wife's family allowed him to travel to America.

Paine found work editing and writing essays for the *Pennsylvania Magazine.* An argument with his boss left him out of work in the fall of 1775. That is when he wrote *Common Sense*, his most famous essay. It was printed and distributed in Philadelphia the following January and spread throughout the colonies with amazing speed.[2] Not everyone agreed with Paine's statements, but there was no doubt that the pamphlet was stirring up the colonists.

Common Sense Convinces

Paine's words were styled for the time he lived in, yet plain enough for anyone from plantation owner to laborer to understand them. His biggest target was the monarchy in England. "There is something exceedingly ridiculous in the composition of the monarchy; it first excludes a man from the means of information, yet empowers him in cases where the highest **judgment** is required."[3] Colonists agreed that

King George III knew nothing about the colonists as people, yet he was making decisions that would change their lives.

"The sun never shined on a cause of greater worth," Paine wrote of the American situation. This kind of talk probably affected people as much as his harsh judgment of the monarchy. They wanted to believe that their cause was **worthy**. Paine ended one section of his pamphlet with these stirring words: "O ye that love mankind! Ye that dare oppose, not only the tyranny, but the tyrant, stand forth!"[4]

Historian Richard Beeman writes, "The publication of *Common Sense* marked a moment when many in America would, in their **zeal** for independence, move well beyond their representatives to the Continental Congress."[5]

The Congress plodded on as it tried to manage the war and the colonies. The Prohibitory Act contained a provision for Britain to send a peace commission to the colonies. As the months dragged on that winter and spring, there was no sign of the promised peace commissioners. John Dickinson saw his last hope for settlement trickling away.

British Troops Leave Boston

Meanwhile, there had been good news on the military front. General Washington had taken Dorchester Heights without a fight on March 4. The new British commander, General William Howe, planned to launch a counterattack but a snowstorm on March 5 stalled his operation. Three days later Howe said his troops would leave Boston if Washington could guarantee their safety. Washington agreed and a starved and depleted Boston was finally free of British troops.

That success helped balance the failure of the Canadian expedition that had begun the previous summer with high hopes. American troops captured Montreal that November,

General George Washington watches as British ships leave Boston Harbor on March 17, 1776. They left after an eight-year British occupation of Boston. Washington's troops had set up fortifications and guns on Dorchester Heights just south of Boston. As a result, the British could no longer defend their positions in Boston. The British fleet fled to Nova Scotia, a British territory.

but the effort to take Quebec City was a disaster. British reinforcements began arriving soon afterward, and the Americans—who had no warm clothing and existed in terrible conditions—were slowly forced back.

Congress made a last-ditch effort in April to salvage the situation by sending three members—Benjamin Franklin, Samuel Chase, and Charles Carroll—to Montreal in hopes that they could persuade the Canadians to support the colonists in their resistance to the British. The mission was unsuccessful.

Despite that setback, Congress had already taken several actions to let the British know that their time in America was short. In February, Congress authorized **privateers** and placed an **embargo** on exports to Britain and the British West Indies. In March, Silas Deane departed to France to negotiate for aid and Congress voted to disarm all loyalists. On April 6, American ports opened to trade with all nations except Britain. Still some delegates waited for the peace commissioners.[6]

The ever-impatient John Adams wrote to his wife in April to voice his opinion of the wait. "This Story of Commissioners is as arrant an Illusion as ever was hatched in the Brain of an Enthusiast, a Politician, or a Maniac. I have laugh'd at it—scolded at it—griev'd at it—and I don't know but I may at an unguarded Moment have rip'd at it, but it is vain to Reason against such Delusions."[7]

John Adams and many other delegates now openly advocated for independence. They hoped to shove the moderates toward action. On May 10, Congress passed a resolution encouraging the colonies to form their own governments if they hadn't already done so. A **preamble** tacked on to the resolution a few days later made clear that the intent was to create governments entirely free of British authority.[8]

Some of the delegates considered this resolution to be a declaration of independence from Great Britain. However, the rest of the delegates weren't ready to say that. It took a few more weeks and a lot more debate before all delegates agreed.

The Committee of Five (from left) John Adams, Roger Sherman, Robert R. Livingston, Thomas Jefferson, and Benjamin Franklin had been appointed to write the Declaration of Independence. They presented it to the Congress on June 28, 1776. The Declaration, with corrections, was approved by the Congress on July 4, 1776.

5

The Great Debate

Delegates who hoped to avoid declaring independence made their final efforts. The Pennsylvania delegates were the most alarmed by the events unfolding. They tried to slow the break with Britain, but it was too late to stop the momentum building for independence.

Virginia had no doubts. Virginia delegate Richard Henry Lee introduced a resolution for independence on June 7. It read in part, "These United Colonies are, and of right ought to be free and independent States, that they are **absolved** from all **allegiance** to the British Crown, and that all political connection between them and the State of Great Britain is, and ought to be, totally dissolved."[1]

Debate started on June 8 and lasted all day and into the night. On June 10, the Congress agreed to delay a vote on the resolution until July 1. The colonial assemblies needed time to instruct their delegates how to vote.

Congress appointed three committees to work during the delay. The most important committee would **frame** the document declaring independence. It consisted of Thomas Jefferson, John Adams, Benjamin Franklin, Roger Sherman, and Robert R. Livingston. Another committee was to prepare a plan for confederation among the colonies, and the third to spell out possible foreign treaties.[2]

Much of the flurry of activity during the second half of June took place outside of the Pennsylvania State House where the delegates met. Riders hurried back and forth to the colonial assemblies to get instructions for voting on Lee's resolution.

The Great Debate

The committee appointed to write the Declaration of Independence met several times over the next few days. They asked Thomas Jefferson to **draft** the document. The committee members read it and suggested changes. The final version of the Declaration went to the Congress at the end of June.

John Adams said that July 1 saw the beginning of "the greatest Debate of all."[3] First Congress had to vote on the postponed resolution that Richard Henry Lee had introduced on June 7. Dickinson began the debate in the early afternoon. He spoke for two hours as he spelled out once again the reasons not to declare independence.

Others may have spoken in favor of independence, but John Adams is the only one whose name was recorded. He spoke passionately that the arguments for independence were clear and had been made many times.[4]

In the late afternoon, the Congress took an unofficial vote on the resolution. The result was nine colonies in favor, two opposed, one colony divided, and another **abstaining**. The Congress voted to postpone the official vote until the next day.

An Historic Vote

Historians feel that some kind of bargaining took place that night after Congress officially adjourned. When the dele-

gates reconvened on July 2, twelve of the thirteen colonies voted to pass Lee's resolution. New York abstained, saying it had not received instructions from its assembly. Dickinson did not show up that day.

John Adams predicted what would happen in years to come to celebrate the occasion, though he was wrong about the date. In a letter to his wife Abigail, Adams said, "The Second Day of July 1776 will be the most memorable **Epoch**, in the history of America. I am apt to believe that it will be celebrated by succeeding Generations, as the great anniversary Festival."

Adams went on to say that the day ought to be celebrated with "Pomp and Parade, with Shews, Games, Sports, Guns, Bells, Bonfires, and Illuminations from one End of the Continent to the other from this Time forward forever more."[5]

On July 3, Congress took up the issue of the Declaration itself. The Congress made many corrections and a few additions to Jefferson's words, and approved it the following day.

The Declaration explained why the colonies thought it was necessary to pull away from Great Britain. It included a long list of grievances against the mother country. The sentence that is most quoted and remembered begins the second paragraph of the Preamble to the Declaration: "We hold these truths to be self-evident, that all men are created equal, that they are **endowed** by their Creator with certain **unalienable** Rights, that among these are Life, Liberty and the pursuit of Happiness."[6]

Spreading the News

Congress ordered that the Declaration be quickly printed and distributed as a broadside. The first official public reading of the Declaration in Philadelphia took place on July 8.

Lieutenant Colonel John Nixon read the Declaration aloud to a crowd in the State House Yard. John Adams described the scene in a letter to Samuel Chase, a delegate from Maryland. "The Batallions paraded on the common, and gave Us the Feu de Joy, notwithstanding the Scarcity of Powder. The Bells rung all Day, and almost all night."[7]

British General William Howe joined the military when he was 17. He fought in the French and Indian War with much success. From his seat in Parliament, he argued against going to war with America. However, he agreed to go with a regiment to America. He said it was his duty and he had no choice.

The delegates had completed the exciting work. The official signing of the Declaration took place on August 2, 1776, after it was properly printed. Congress had reached the high point of the last few years. However, the delegates still had a war to run so they could not travel home to celebrate.

In an unexpected twist, two high-ranking British officers who were brothers arrived in New York just over a week after Congress declared independence. General William Howe commanded thousands of soldiers, while Admiral Richard Howe commanded dozens of warships and transports carrying his brother's troops. While their primary purpose was to take control of the city, the brothers believed that they might also negotiate an end to the conflict and appeared to be the long-awaited peace commissioners.

Their military campaign began in late August when they defeated Washington and captured Long Island. Washington withdrew his troops to Manhattan Island.

A Faint Hope Quickly Dashed

Soon afterward, Richard Howe offered to meet with representatives of Congress to discuss the possibility of ending the conflict. What became known as the Staten Island Peace Conference took place on September 11 and lasted for several hours. The Americans soon realized that Howe had almost no power to negotiate anything substantial with them. All he had to offer were royal pardons for those willing to say they were sorry for having supported the rebel cause.[8]

With the failure of the talks, the British renewed their attacks on Washington's troops on Manhattan. After a series of defeats, Washington withdrew all his forces from New York and the surrounding area, then crossed the Hudson River and retreated toward Philadelphia. The British pursued them.

Despite Washington's victory at Trenton on Christmas Day, he couldn't stop the British as they drove toward Philadelphia. Congress adjourned to Baltimore, Maryland, though eventually they returned to Philadelphia.

Despite the disruption, they continued with their business. The work of the confederation committee was especially important. But the colonies were new at working together and couldn't agree on several items. Should the states each have one vote, or should states with larger populations have more votes? Should only men with property be able to vote? Should slaves be counted as part of the population of a state?

After well over a year of debate, the committee produced the Articles of Confederation in late 1777. All 13

German artist Emanuel Leutze painted "Washington Crossing the Delaware" in 1851. Washington needed a victory to boost morale among his troops. On Christmas Eve, 1776, he and his men crossed the storm-tossed Delaware river. The following morning they launched a surprise attack on enemy troops stationed around Trenton, New Jersey. The attack was successful, with over 1,000 enemy troops captured.

states had to approve them before they could come into effect. More than three years went by before Maryland became the 13th and final state to approve them. The Articles were officially adopted on March 1, 1781. The Second Continental Congress formally ended. It was immediately replaced by the United States in Congress Assembled. The new body retained the same membership. As a result, many people continued to call it the Continental Congress. Either way, it became the governing body of the United States. But its inability to effectively deal with the many problems facing the new nation led to the adoption of the Constitution eight years later. The United States

Congress and the executive branch headed by the president succeeded it.

Despite its faults, the Second Continental Congress had achieved something of supreme importance. It created the United States of America.

British general Lord Cornwallis surrendered his army at Yorktown, Virginia, on October 19, 1781. It was the last major action of the Revolutionary War. The United States in Congress Assembled was responsible for conducting the complicated peace negotiations that ended in the Treaty of Paris. Signed on September 3, 1783, it ended the war.

APPENDIX 1

DELEGATES TO THE SECOND CONTINENTAL CONGRESS

John Adams (1735-1826) was a Massachusetts delegate to both the First and Second Continental Congresses. Adams was later elected the first vice president of the United States and served as president from 1797 through 1801.

Samuel Adams (1722-1803) was a Massachusetts delegate to the Continental Congresses from 1774-1781. He was one of the Sons of Liberty who first agitated for independence. He signed the Declaration of Independence and later was governor of Massachusetts.

Samuel Chase (1741-1811) of Maryland was a member of both Congresses and was sent on a special mission in 1776 to try to obtain Canadian support. He signed the Declaration of Independence and became an associate justice of the U.S. Supreme Court in 1796.

Silas Deane (1737-1789) was a delegate from Connecticut who served in both Continental Congresses. Congress sent him to France in March 1776 as a secret political and financial agent. He helped to negotiate the treaty between France and the United States in 1778 and secured the services of the Marquis de Lafayette and other foreign military officers.

John Dickinson (1732-1808) was a delegate from Pennsylvania during the First and Second Continental Congresses. He later represented Delaware when he signed the Articles of Confederation and the Constitution. Dickinson argued passionately for a peaceful solution to the breach with Great Britain. Seeing that he had failed in this objective, he didn't attend the session approving the Declaration of Independence and did not sign it.

Benjamin Franklin (1706-1790) of Pennsylvania was the oldest member of the Second Continental Congress and the best-known. Many of his accomplishments took place before the revolution. He signed the Declaration of Independence and served as Minister to France from 1776-1785. Franklin was one of the negotiators of the peace treaty with Great Britain.

John Hancock (1737-1793) of Massachusetts was president of the Congress from 1775-1777. He was the first signer of the Declaration of Independence. He served as senior major general of the Massachusetts Militia during the war and was governor of Massachusetts from 1780-1785.

John Jay (1745-1829) of New York served five years in the Continental Congresses but did not sign the Declaration of Independence. He signed the Treaty of Paris and served as Secretary of Foreign Affairs. He was the first chief justice of the U.S. Supreme Court and governor of New York 1795-1801.

Thomas Jefferson (1743-1826) served in the Second Continental Congress and is credited with writing the Declaration of Independence. Later he was governor of Virginia, U.S. secretary of state, vice president, and president from 1801 to 1809.

APPENDIX 1

DELEGATES TO THE SECOND CONTINENTAL CONGRESS

Richard Henry Lee (1732-1794) was a Virginia delegate to both Continental Congresses. He introduced the resolution for independence and signed the Declaration. He was a colonel of the Westmoreland Militia and later served in the U.S. Senate.

Robert R. Livingston (1746-1813) served in the Second Continental Congress for five years as a New York delegate. He was on the committee to draft the Declaration of Independence but returned to duties in the New York provincial assembly before signing the document. Later he was Secretary of Foreign Affairs and was Robert Fulton's partner in constructing the first steamboat.

Thomas Mifflin (1744-1800) of Pennsylvania served in both Continental Congresses. He was an aide to General Washington and rose to the rank of major general before resigning in 1779. He was a delegate to the Federal Constitutional Convention in 1787.

Robert Morris (1734-1806) of Pennsylvania served in the Second Continental Congress and signed the Declaration of Independence. One of the richest men in America, he became known as the "financier of the American Revolution." He was a U.S. senator from 1789 until 1795.

Robert Treat Paine (1731-1814) of Massachusetts served in both Continental Congresses and signed the Declaration of Independence. Later he was attorney general of Massachusetts and delegate to the state's constitutional convention in 1779.

Peyton Randoph (1721-1775) of Virginia served in both Congresses and was president until his sudden death on October 22, 1775. Earlier he had been chairman of the Virginia Committee of Correspondence.

Caesar Rodney (1728-1784) served in both Congresses as a Delaware delegate and signed the Declaration of Independence. He was a brigadier general in the Continental Army and later elected president of Delaware.

Benjamin Rush (1746-1813) of Pennsylvania served in the Second Continental Congress and signed the Declaration of Independence. Rush was a physician who served in several positions during the war. Later he founded the Pennsylvania Hospital in Philadelphia and was treasurer of the U.S. Mint from 1799 until his death in 1813.

Roger Sherman (1721-1793) was a Connecticut delegate and the only member of the Continental Congresses who signed all four major U.S. historical documents: the Association of 1774, the Declaration of Independence, the Articles of Confederation, and the Constitution.

George Washington (1732-1799) of Virginia served in both Congresses and was appointed commander-in-chief of the Continental Army in June 1775. He held this position until 1783. In 1789 Washington became the first president of the United States. He served until 1797. In 1798 he was appointed lieutenant general and commander of the U.S. Army in anticipation of a possible war with France.

APPENDIX 2

ORIGINAL SOURCE DOCUMENTS

IN CONGRESS, JULY 4, 1776.

The unanimous Declaration of the thirteen united States of America,

When in the Course of human events, it becomes necessary for one people to dissolve the political bands which have connected them with another, and to assume among the powers of the earth, the separate and equal station to which the Laws of Nature and of Nature's God entitle them, a decent respect to the opinions of mankind requires that they should declare the causes which impel them to the separation. —— We hold these truths to be self-evident, that all men are created equal, that they are endowed by their Creator with certain unalienable Rights, that among these are Life, Liberty and the pursuit of Happiness. — That to secure these rights, Governments are instituted among Men, deriving their just powers from the consent of the governed, — That whenever any Form of Government becomes destructive of these ends, it is the Right of the People to alter or to abolish it, and to institute new Government, laying its foundation on such principles and organizing its powers in such form, as to them shall seem most likely to effect their Safety and Happiness. Prudence, indeed, will dictate that Governments long established should not be changed for light and transient causes; and accordingly all experience hath shewn, that mankind are more disposed to suffer, while evils are sufferable, than to right themselves by abolishing the forms to which they are accustomed. But when a long train of abuses and usurpations, pursuing invariably the same Object evinces a design to reduce them under absolute Despotism, it is their right, it is their duty, to throw off such Government, and to provide new Guards for their future security. — Such has been the patient sufferance of these Colonies; and such is now the necessity which constrains them to alter their former Systems of Government. The history of the present King of Great Britain is a history of repeated injuries and usurpations, all having in direct object the establishment of an absolute Tyranny over these States. To prove this, let Facts be submitted to a candid world. —— He has refused his Assent to Laws, the most wholesome and necessary for the public good. —— He has forbidden his Governors to pass Laws of immediate and pressing importance, unless suspended in their operation till his Assent should be obtained; and when so suspended, he has utterly neglected to attend to them. —— He has refused to pass other Laws for the accommodation of large districts of people, unless those people would relinquish the right of Representation in the Legislature, a right inestimable to them and formidable to tyrants only. —— He has called together legislative bodies at places unusual, uncomfortable, and distant from the depository of their public Records, for the sole purpose of fatiguing them into compliance with his measures. —— He has dissolved Representative Houses repeatedly, for opposing with manly firmness his invasions on the rights of the people. —— He has refused for a long time, after such dissolutions, to cause others to be elected; whereby the Legislative powers, incapable of Annihilation, have returned to the People at large for their exercise; the State remaining in the mean time exposed to all the dangers of invasion from without, and convulsions within. —— He has endeavoured to prevent the population of these States; for that purpose obstructing the Laws for Naturalization of Foreigners; refusing to pass others to encourage their migrations hither, and raising the conditions of new Appropriations of Lands. —— He has obstructed the Administration of Justice, by refusing his Assent to Laws for establishing Judiciary powers. —— He has made Judges dependent on his Will alone, for the tenure of their offices, and the amount and payment of their salaries. —— He has erected a multitude of New Offices, and sent hither swarms of Officers to harrass our people, and eat out their substance. —— He has kept among us, in times of peace, Standing Armies without the Consent of our legislatures. —— He has affected to render the Military independent of and superior to the Civil power. —— He has combined with others to subject us to a jurisdiction foreign to our constitution, and unacknowledged by our laws; giving his Assent to their Acts of pretended Legislation: —— For Quartering large bodies of armed troops among us: —— For protecting them, by a mock Trial, from punishment for any Murders which they should commit on the Inhabitants of these States: —— For cutting off our Trade with all parts of the world: —— For imposing Taxes on us without our Consent: —— For depriving us in many cases, of the benefits of Trial by Jury: —— For transporting us beyond Seas to be tried for pretended offences —— For abolishing the free System of English Laws in a neighbouring Province, establishing therein an Arbitrary government, and enlarging its Boundaries so as to render it at once an example and fit instrument for introducing the same absolute rule into these Colonies: —— For taking away our Charters, abolishing our most valuable Laws, and altering fundamentally the Forms of our Governments: —— For suspending our own Legislatures, and declaring themselves invested with power to legislate for us in all cases whatsoever. —— He has abdicated Government here, by declaring us out of his Protection and waging War against us. —— He has plundered our seas, ravaged our Coasts, burnt our towns, and destroyed the lives of our people. —— He is at this time transporting large Armies of foreign Mercenaries to compleat the works of death, desolation and tyranny, already begun with circumstances of Cruelty & perfidy scarcely paralleled in the most barbarous ages, and totally unworthy the Head of a civilized nation. —— He has constrained our fellow Citizens taken Captive on the high Seas to bear Arms against their Country, to become the executioners of their friends and Brethren, or to fall themselves by their Hands. —— He has excited domestic insurrections amongst us, and has endeavoured to bring on the inhabitants of our frontiers, the merciless Indian Savages, whose known rule of warfare, is an undistinguished destruction of all ages, sexes and conditions. In every stage of these Oppressions We have Petitioned for Redress in the most humble terms: Our repeated Petitions have been answered only by repeated injury. A Prince, whose character is thus marked by every act which may define a Tyrant, is unfit to be the ruler of a free people. Nor have We been wanting in attentions to our Brittish brethren. We have warned them from time to time of attempts by their legislature to extend an unwarrantable jurisdiction over us. We have reminded them of the circumstances of our emigration and settlement here. We have appealed to their native justice and magnanimity, and we have conjured them by the ties of our common kindred to disavow these usurpations, which, would inevitably interrupt our connections and correspondence. They too have been deaf to the voice of justice and of consanguinity. We must, therefore, acquiesce in the necessity, which denounces our Separation, and hold them, as we hold the rest of mankind, Enemies in War, in Peace Friends. ——

We, therefore, the Representatives of the united States of America, in General Congress, Assembled, appealing to the Supreme Judge of the world for the rectitude of our intentions, do, in the Name, and by Authority of the good People of these Colonies, solemnly publish and declare, That these United Colonies are, and of Right ought to be Free and Independent States; that they are Absolved from all Allegiance to the British Crown, and that all political connection between them and the State of Great Britain, is and ought to be totally dissolved; and that as Free and Independent States, they have full Power to levy War, conclude Peace, contract Alliances, establish Commerce, and to do all other Acts and Things which Independent States may of right do. —— And for the support of this Declaration, with a firm reliance on the protection of divine Providence, we mutually pledge to each other our Lives, our Fortunes and our sacred Honor.

John Hancock

Button Gwinnett
Lyman Hall
Geo Walton.

Wm Hooper
Joseph Hewes,
John Penn

Edward Rutledge.

Thos Heyward Junr.
Thomas Lynch Junr.
Arthur Middleton

Samuel Chase
Wm. Paca
Thos. Stone
Charles Carroll of Carrollton

George Wythe
Richard Henry Lee
Th Jefferson
Benja. Harrison
Thos Nelson jr.
Francis Lightfoot Lee
Carter Braxton

Robt Morris
Benjamin Rush
Benja. Franklin
John Morton
Geo Clymer
Jas. Smith
Geo. Taylor
James Wilson
Geo. Ross
Caesar Rodney
Geo Read
Tho M:Kean

Wm Floyd
Phil. Livingston
Frans. Lewis
Lewis Morris
Richd. Stockton
Jno Witherspoon
Fras. Hopkinson
John Hart
Abra Clark

Josiah Bartlett
Wm. Whipple
Saml Adams
John Adams
Robt Treat Paine
Elbridge Gerry
Step. Hopkins
William Ellery
Roger Sherman
Saml Huntington
Wm. Williams
Oliver Wolcott
Matthew Thornton

https://www.archives.gov/publications/prologue/2003/fall/stone-engraving.html

APPENDIX 2

ORIGINAL SOURCE DOCUMENTS

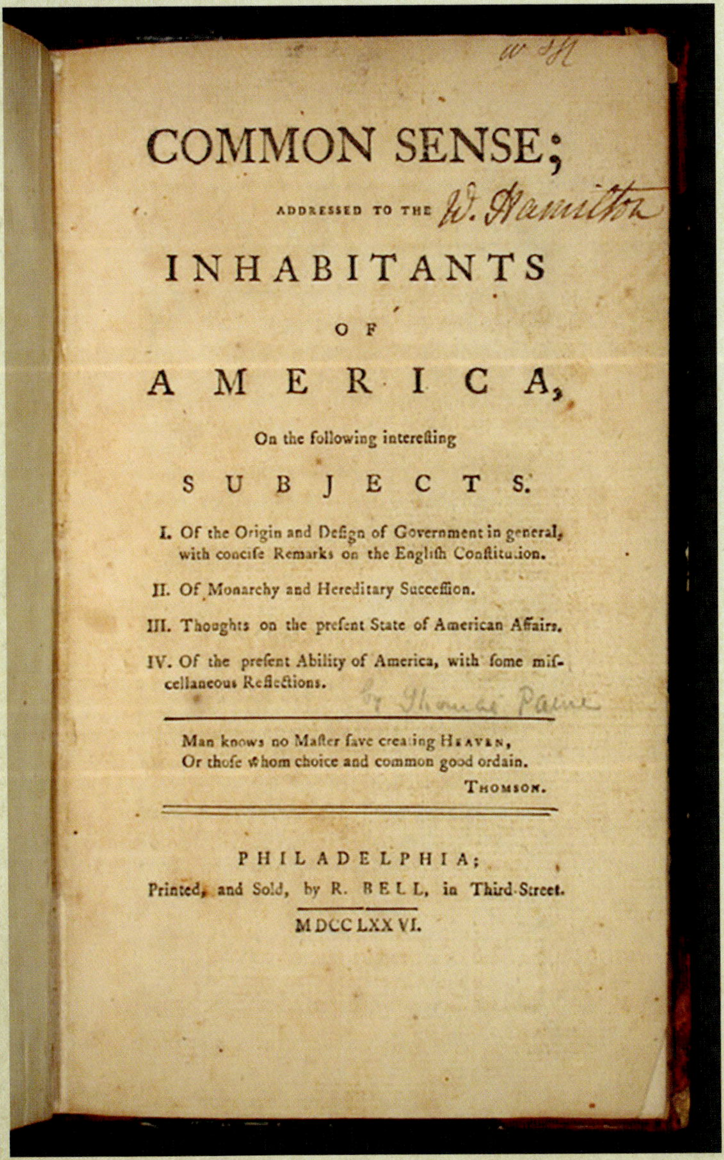

COMMON SENSE;

ADDRESSED TO THE

INHABITANTS

OF

AMERICA,

On the following interesting

SUBJECTS.

I. Of the Origin and Design of Government in general, with concise Remarks on the English Constitution.

II. Of Monarchy and Hereditary Succession.

III. Thoughts on the present State of American Affairs.

IV. Of the present Ability of America, with some miscellaneous Reflections.

> Man knows no Master save creating HEAVEN,
> Or those whom choice and common good ordain.
>
> THOMSON.

PHILADELPHIA;
Printed, and Sold, by R. BELL, in Third-Street.
MDCCLXXVI.

http://www.indiana.edu/~liblilly/history/common-sense.html

CHAPTER NOTES

Chapter 1: Stamp Acts and Tea Parties

1. Edmund Cody Burnett, *The Continental Congress* (New York: W.W. Norton, 1964), pp. 7-8.
2. Ibid., p. 11.
3. Richard R. Beeman, *Our Sacred Honor: The Forging of American Independence, 1774-1776* (New York: Basic Books, 2013), pp. 22-25.
4. Burnett, pp. 17-18.
5. Lynn Montross, *The Reluctant Rebels: The Story of the Continental Congress, 1774-1789* (New York: Alfred A. Knopf, 1979), p. 25.
6. Beeman, pp. 149, 165-169.
7. L.H. Butterfield, editor, *Diary and Autobiography of John Adams, Volume 2, Diary 1771-1781* (New York: Atheneum, 1964), p. 157.

Chapter 2: Return to Philadelphia

1. Worthington C. Ford et. al., editors, *The Journals of the Continental Congress, 1774-1789*, Volume 1 (Washington, DC: Library of Congress, 1904-1937), pp. 120-121.
2. Henry Steele Commager and Richard B. Morris, eds., *The Spirit of 'Seventy-Six: The Story of the American Revolution as Told by Participants* (New York: HarperCollins, 1958), p. 61.
3. Paul Smith et. al., editors, *Letters of Delegates to Congress, 1774-1789*, Volume 1 (Washington, DC: Library of Congress, 1976-2000), pp. 351-352.
4. Ibid., pp. 371-383.
5. Richard Beeman, *Our Lives, Our Fortunes and Our Sacred Honor: The Forging of American Independence, 1774-1776* (New York: Basic Books, 2013), pp. 239-241.
6. Ford, Volume 2, p. 127.

Chapter 3: Running the War

1. Edmund Burnett, *The Continental Congress* (New York: W.W. Norton, 1964), pp. 93, 97-99.
2. Paul Smith et. al., editors, *Letters of Delegates to Congress, 1774-1789*, Volume 1 (Washington, DC: Library of Congress, 1976-2000), p. 674.
3. Richard Beeman, *Our Lives, Our Fortunes and Our Sacred Honor: The Forging of American Independence, 1774-1776* (New York: Basic Books, 2013), p. 263.
4. Ibid., p. 262.
5. Ibid., pp. 267-269.
6. Ibid., pp. 276-277.
7. Ibid., pp. 291-292.

CHAPTER NOTES

Chapter 4: "Common Sense" Persuades

1. Richard Beeman, *Our Lives, Our Fortunes and Our Sacred Honor: The Forging of American Independence, 1774-1776* (New York: Basic Books, 2013), pp. 301-303.

2. Ibid., pp. 305-311.

3. Thomas Paine, *Common Sense.* http://www.gutenberg.org/files/147/147-h/147-h.htm, p. 6.

4. Ibid., p. 23.

5. Beeman, p. 327.

6. Henry Steele Commager and Richard B. Morris, editors, *The Spirit of 'Seventy-Six: The Story of the American Revolution as Told by Participants* (New York: HarperCollins, 1958), p. 292.

7. L.H. Butterfield, editor, *Adams Family Correspondence, Volume 2, Diary 1771-1781* (Cambridge, MA: Harvard University Press, 1963), pp. 383-385.

8. Beeman, p. 345.

Chapter 5: The Great Debate

1. Richard R. Beeman, *Our Lives, Our Fortunes and Our Sacred Honor: The Forging of American Independence, 1774-1776* (New York: Basic Books, 2013), p. 351.

2. Edmund Burnett, *The Continental Congress* (New York: W.W. Norton, 1964), p. 173.

3. Robert Taylor, et al., editors, *Papers of John Adams*, Volume 4 (Cambridge, MA: Harvard University Press, 1977), pp. 345-347.

4. Beeman, p. 374.

5. L.H. Butterfield, editor, *Adams Family Correspondence, Volume 2, Diary 1771-1781* (Cambridge, MA: Harvard University Press, 1963), pp. 27-31.

6. Declaration of Independence, National Archives http://www.archives.gov/exhibits/charters/declaration.html

7. Robert J. Taylor, et al., editors, *Papers of John Adams*, Volume 9 (Cambridge, MA: Harvard University Press, 1977), p. 372.

8. Jack Rakove, *The Beginnings of National Politics: An Interpretive History of the Continental Congress* (New York: Alfred A. Knopf, 1979), p. 112.

9. Burnett, pp. 223-229.

FURTHER READING

Allen, Thomas. *George Washington, Spymaster: How the Americans Outspied the British and Won the Revolutionary War*. Des Moines, IA: National Geographic Children's Books, 2007.

Brooks, Phillip. *King George III: America's Enemy* (Wicked History). New York: Franklin Watts, 2009.

Burnett, Betty. *The Continental Congress: A Primary Source History of the Formation of America's New Government*. New York: Rosen, 2004.

Conklin, Wendy. *Early Congresses* (Primary Source Readers). Westminster, CA: Teacher Created Materials, 2004.

Freedman, Russell. *The Boston Tea Party*. New York: Holiday House, 2013.

Kelley, True. *Who Was Abigail Adams?* New York: Grosset & Dunlap, 2014.

Kjelle, Marylou Morano. *The First Continental Congress*. Hallandale, FL: Mitchell Lane Publishers, 2018.

Ransom, Candace. *What Was the Continental Congress?: And Other Questions about the Declaration of Independence* (Six Questions of American History). Minneapolis, MN: Lerner Classroom, 2011.

WORKS CONSULTED

Adams Family Correspondence, Vols. 1-10. Cambridge, MA: Harvard University Press, 1963.

Beeman, Richard R. *Our Lives, Our Fortunes and Our Sacred Honor: The Forging of American Independence, 1774-1776*. New York: Basic Books, 2013.

Bicheno, Hugh. *Rebels & Redcoats; The American Revolutionary War*. London: HarperCollins, 2003.

Burnett, Edmund Cody. *The Continental Congress*. New York: W.W. Norton, 1964.

Butterfield, L.H., editor. *Diary and Autobiography of John Adams: Volume 2, Diary* 1771-1781. New York: Atheneum, 1964.

Commager, Henry Steele and Richard B. Morris, editors. *The Spirit of 'Seventy-Six: The Story of the American Revolution as Told by Participants*. New York: HarperCollins, 1958.

Declaration of Independence, National Archives. http://www.archives.gov/exhibits/charters/declaration.html

Ferling, John. *John Adams: A Life*. Knoxville, TN: The University of Tennessee Press, 1992.

Ford, Worthington C. et. al., editors. *The Journals of the Continental Congress, 1774-1789*, Volume 1. Washington, DC: Library of Congress, 1904-1937.

WORKS CONSULTED

Fowler, William M., Jr. *Samuel Adams: Radical Puritan*. New York: Longman, 1997.

Marston, Jerrilyn Greene. *King and Congress: The Transfer of Political Legitimacy, 1774-1776*. Princeton, NJ: Princeton University Press, 1987.

McCullough, David. *John Adams*. New York: Simon & Schuster, 2001.

Meigs, Cornelia. *The Violent Men: A Study of Human Relations in the First American Congress*. New York: The Macmillan Company, 1950.

Montross, Lynn. *The Reluctant Rebels: The Story of the Continental Congress, 1774-1789*. New York: Barnes & Noble, 1970.

Paine, Thomas. *Common Sense*. http://www.gutenberg.org/files/147/147-h/147-h.htm

Rakove, Jack. *The Beginnings of National Politics: An Interpretive History of the Continental Congress*. New York: Alfred A. Knopf, 1979.

Schlesinger, Arthur Meier. *The Colonial Merchants and the American Revolution, 1763-1776*. New York: Frederick Ungar, 1957.

Smith, Paul H. et. al., eds. *Letters of Delegates to Congress, 1774-1789*. 29 volumes. Washington, DC: Library of Congress, 1976-2000.

Taylor, Robert J. et. al. editors. *Papers of John Adams*. Volumes 1-16. Cambridge, MA: Harvard University Press, 1977.

PHOTO CREDITS: All design elements from Thinkstock/Sharon Beck. Cover, p. 30—John Trumbull/US Capitol/Public Domain; p. 4—Johann Zoffany/The Royal Collection/Public Domain; pp. 7, 15, 23, 37—Library of Congress; p. 9—US Capitol/public domain; p. 10— John Singleton Copley/CC0 1.0/Public Domain; p. 12, 18, 28—North Wind Picture Archives/ Alamy Stock Photo; p. 13–National Portrait Gallery, Washington, DC/Billy Hathorn/cc by-sa 3.0; p. 16—Howard Pyle/ Public Domain; p. 21—Niday Picture Library/Alamy Stock Photo; p. 24—Laurent Dabos/National Portrait Gallery/public domain; p. 34—Richard Purcell aka Charles Corbutt/Public Domain; p. 36—Emanuel Leutze/Metropolitan Museum of Art/ Public Domain; p. 40—National Archives and Records Administration; p. 41—Indiana.edu/Public Domain.

GLOSSARY

absolved (ab-SOLV-ed)—declared free from guilt or blame
abstaining (ab-STAYN-ing)—holding back from something, such as voting neither yes or no
allegiance (ah-LEE-jens)—duty owed to a leader or government
avowed (ah-VOWD)—to openly admit to a claim or action to be taken
boycott (BOI-caht)—a ban on purchases from a particular organization as a form of protest
broadside (BRAWD-side)—a large sheet of paper printed on one side
chronic (KRAHN-ik)—lasting a long time or recurring often
confiscated (KAHN-fis-cay-ted)—seized or took over; usually by an authority
convened (kan-VEEND)—met together
draft (DRAFT)—write a preliminary sketch
embargo (em-BAHR-go)—a government order prohibiting the entry or departure of ships at a port
endowed (en-DOWD)—provided with some quality or talent
epoch (EH-pahk)—a period of time characterized by noteworthy events
fifes (FIFES)—small flutes with six or eight finger holes
fortifications (for-tif-uh-KAY-shuns)—forts, walls, or earthworks used to strengthen a position
frame (FRAME)—shape or put together the parts of something
grievances (GREV-unhn-suhz)—complaints about circumstances thought to be unfair
incompetent (in-KOM-puh-tent)—lacking knowledge or ability; incapable
intolerable (in-TOHL-er-uh-buhl)—too severe or painful to be endured
judgment (JUDG-ment)—opinion about something
marines (ma-RENS)—soldiers capable of fighting both on land and at sea
monopoly (muh-NAW-puh-lee)—exclusive control of a product or service
munitions (myoo-NISH-enzs)—weapons or ammunition
preamble (PRE-am-buhl)—written introduction to a document, stating the reasons and purposes for that document
privateers (pry-vuh-TEARS)--privately owned ships hired by a government to attack and capture enemy ships
prohibitions (pro-uh-BISH-ens)—laws that forbid something
reconciliation (reh-cuhn-sill-ee-A-shun)—the settling of a difference of opinion
recruitment (ree-KROOT-ment)—persuading people to enlist in an army or navy
repealed (ree-PEELD)— canceled or withdrew
resolve (ree-ZOLV)—a firm purpose
restrictions (ree-STRIK-shuns)—limitations placed on actions
sequel (SEE-kwel)—something that follows; a book or movie that comes after an earlier version
smuggled (SMUG-gled)— to bring goods or people into a country secretly and usually illegally
unalienable (un-AYL-ee-un-able)—not capable of being transferred; innate
worthy (WUR-thee)—deserving of something
zeal (ZEEL)—intense devotion to something

INDEX

About the Author

Bonnie Hinman has published more than 40 books, most of them nonfiction. Several of her books have focused on the founding years of the United States. The American Revolution with its strong men and women has always fascinated her. Reading the primary documents gave her a new window into the world of those Americans. Fireworks on the Fourth of July have new meaning for Bonnie since she read John Adams' letter to his wife, declaring that independence should be celebrated with "illuminations." Bonnie graduated from Missouri State University and lives in Joplin, Missouri, with her husband Bill and near her children and five grandchildren.